STONEWALL JACKSON'S
BLACK SUNDAY SCHOOL

STONEWALL JACKSON'S
BLACK SUNDAY SCHOOL

By Rickey E. Pittman

Illustrated by
Lynn Hosegood

PELICAN PUBLISHING COMPANY
GRETNA 2010

To Declan, Brynn, and Camden
—L. H.

*The word "Pelican" and the depiction of a pelican
are trademarks of Pelican Publishing Company, Inc.,
and are registered in the U.S. Patent and Trademark Office.*

Library of Congress Cataloging-in-Publication Data

Pittman, Rickey.
  Stonewall Jackson's Black Sunday school / by Rickey E. Pittman ; illustrated by Lynn Hosegood.
    p. cm.
  ISBN 978-1-58980-713-6 (alk. paper)
 1. Jackson, Stonewall, 1824-1863—Relations with slaves. 2. Jackson, Stonewall, 1824-1863—Relations with free African Americans. 3. Jackson, Stonewall, 1824-1863—Relations with African Americans. 4. Generals—Confederate States of America—Biography. 5. Sunday school teachers—Virginia—Lexington—Biography. 6. Slaves—Virginia—Lexington—History—19th century. 7. Free African Americans—Virginia—Lexington—History—19th century. 8. African Americans—Virginia—Lexington—History—19th century. 9. Lexington (Va.)—Race relations—History—19th century. I. Hosegood, Lynn, ill. II. Title.
  E467.1.J15P58 2010
  973.7'3092—dc22
                    2009030285

Printed in Singapore
Published by Pelican Publishing Company, Inc.
1000 Burmaster Street, Gretna, Louisiana 70053

Autumn 1855

When the church bells rang at 2:45 P.M. on Sunday afternoons, people in the town of Lexington, Virginia, made their way in wagons, carriages, on horseback, and on foot to worship. However, this Sunday was a special day in Lexington's history because among the many worshipers were people of color—servants and free men, women, and children of all ages. They were making their way to the Lexington Presbyterian Church to attend Sunday school.

At 3:00 P.M., Thomas J. Jackson, a professor at the Virginia Military Institute, would be the first superintendent of this Sunday school. He walked into the lecture hall where the class would be held. Professor Jackson welcomed the crowd and then said, "All men need to be taught the way of salvation. However, I cannot make you come to school and learn. Are you willing to be taught and come to school every week?"

The room was full of people who were excited to be given the opportunity to worship and be taught the Bible. They all replied, "We are willing, Professor. Give us a Sunday school!"

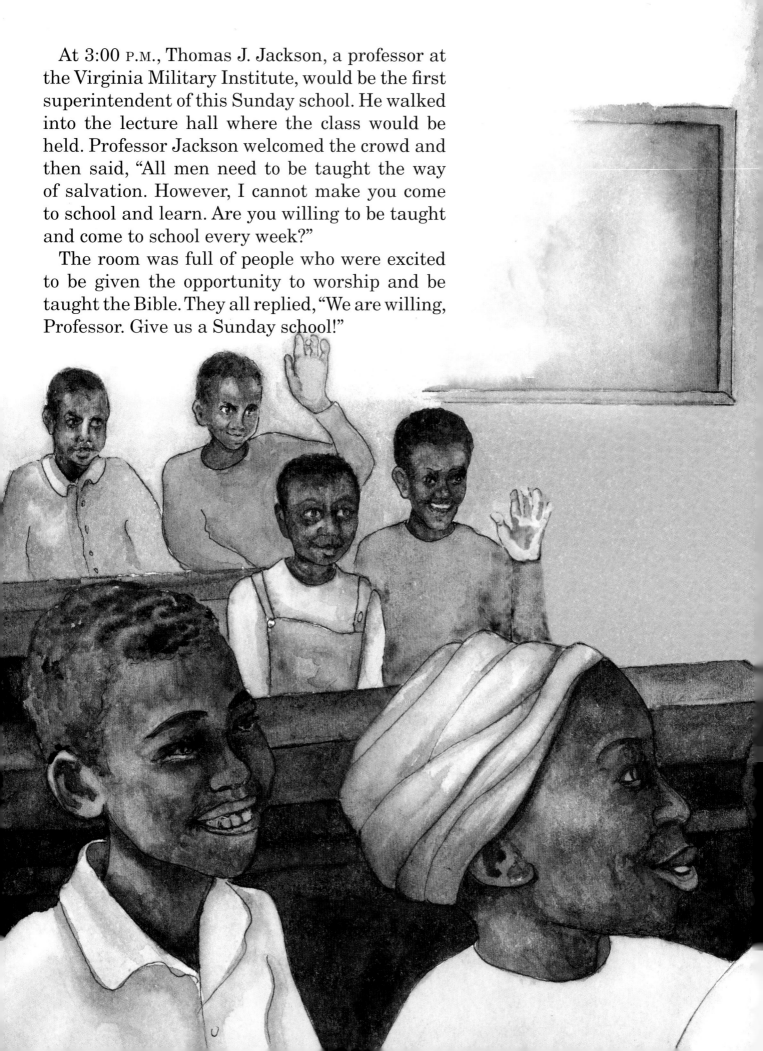

For many years, Virginia law had long declared it illegal for blacks to assemble in groups for instruction in reading and writing, so opportunities like this one were rare. Those who violated the law risked ridicule, fines, and imprisonment. Many slave traders in the North and slaveholders in both the North and South did not think black Americans were as capable of instruction as white Americans. However, times were changing, and Professor Jackson believed all men, no matter what their race, should be taught the way of God. He was determined to teach these Lexington citizens the Bible—even if it was against the law.

Professor Jackson always wore his blue military jacket buttoned to the top even on the hottest day. The students loved and respected him, though it was hard for them not to smile when he sang, because he was always off key. In the beginning, the teaching was oral, as very few blacks in those days had learned to read. But Thomas J. Jackson diligently taught his young and old scholars to read and write. He wanted them to become better men and women through education.

He and the other teachers kept attendance records, and students with good attendance were rewarded. Professor Jackson showed interest in and prayed for every student. Starting promptly at 3:00 P.M., the class door would be locked, and no one dared be late.

The students were taught lessons on the life of Jesus, the parables, the miracles, Old Testament history, the Ten Commandments, the Lord's Prayer, and the Apostles' Creed. Each week, the number of Sunday school members increased. Eventually, the Sunday school obtained an organ, and talented musicians from town performed the service music every week.

However, not all of Lexington's citizens approved of Jackson's Sunday school. Once, two lawyers threatened him with criminal prosecution, saying, "You are breaking the law." Professor Jackson responded to one of them, "Sir, if you were a Christian man, you would not think or say so."

Thomas J. Jackson's belief that the gospel should be taught to all men kept these threats from discouraging him. He worked with the Rockbridge Bible Society, whose mission was to spread the word of God, to raise money for Bibles and literature for the members of his Sunday school. Many free blacks in Lexington were the first to contribute. On the first Sunday of each month, Professor Jackson rewarded his most diligent and loyal students with these gifts.

When the War Between the States began in 1861, Professor Jackson left Lexington with cadets from the military institute to join the Confederate Army. He said goodbye to his Sunday school scholars. Many of them shed tears. Though they would miss him, Professor Jackson would miss them just as much.

During the war, his troops won several battles. The professor proved himself such a great army leader that he became known as "Stonewall Jackson." General Jackson and his horse, Little Sorrel, were known and loved throughout the South.

One day, Reverend White, a Presbyterian pastor in Lexington, received a letter from General Jackson. A great crowd gathered around him, all of them eager for news of the war and General Jackson's victories. As he opened the letter, he said, "Now we shall know the facts about the war." The letter stated:

My Dear Pastor:

In my tent last night, I remembered that I had failed to send you my contribution for our colored Sunday school. Enclosed you will find my check for fifty dollars.

Yours faithfully,
T. J. Jackson

During the war, General Jackson continued to pray for the members of the Sunday school in Lexington. In camp, one could often see a white handkerchief hanging on the outside of his tent. This meant that Jackson was in prayer and was not to be disturbed.

On May 2, 1863, General Jackson was accidentally wounded. He had prayed all his life to die on the Sabbath, and he died on Sunday, May 10.

Special funeral services were held to honor him in Richmond. Afterwards, his coffin was taken to Lexington, where he was buried in the Presbyterian church's cemetery on May 15. Jim Lewis, General Jackson's personal servant, was given the honor of leading the riderless Little Sorrel in both funerals. Everyone in Lexington was saddened by the news of Jackson's death.

Those who attended the Sunday school in Lexington would never forget Professor Jackson. After the Federal Army occupied Lexington at the end of the war, visitors to the church's cemetery found a small Confederate flag on Jackson's grave. The flag had a gospel hymn pinned to it. A young boy who had attended Jackson's Sunday school had placed the small memorial on his grave during the night.

Because of Professor Jackson's work at the Sunday school, three black churches were created in Lexington, and a good number of Professor Jackson's students became members of those churches. Many of his students and their children would later become important community leaders, ministers, and educators. They contributed liberally to the statue that was erected at Professor Jackson's grave.

One of these leaders was Lylburn Liggins Downing, pastor of the Fifth Avenue Presbyterian Church in Roanoke, Virginia. His parents had attended Jackson's Sunday school. Determined to honor Professor Jackson, Downing designed and raised money for a beautiful stained-glass window in honor of Jackson. Many Americans travel to this church every year to see the window. Jackson's last words are inscribed at the bottom of the window:

"Let us cross over the river and rest in the shade of the trees."

Stonewall Jackson Timeline

*The events included here are meant to serve as talking points with children.

1824: Thomas J. Jackson born in Clarksburg, Virginia.

1826: Jackson's father dies.

1831: Jackson's mother dies.

1842: Admitted to West Point. He graduates in 1846, seventeenth out of a class of sixty with the rank of second lieutenant of artillery.

1847: Fights in the Mexican War and is promoted to brevet major.

1848: Baptized and makes public profession of faith.

1850: Served in the army in Florida.

1851: Appointed professor of artillery tactics and natural philosophy at the Virginia Military Institute. Joins the Lexington Presbyterian Church.

1853: Marries Elinor "Ellie" Junkin.

1854: Jackson's wife and infant die during childbirth.

1855: Jackson and VMI cadets follow radical abolitionist John Brown to the gallows in Charlestown, Virginia (now West Virginia).

1861: On April 21, Jackson leaves Lexington to serve in the Confederate Army. He is promoted to brigadier general.

1863: Jackson is mistakenly shot by sentries on May 2 and dies on May 10.

1906: A stained-glass window honoring Jackson was designed by Lylburn L. Downing, an attendee of Jackson's Sunday school as a child. Later, as a pastor, he had the window installed at the Fifth Avenue Presbyterian Church in Roanoke, Virginia.

Stonewall Jackson Facts

- Stonewall Jackson appeared on the Confederate States of America $500 bill (seventh issue, February 17, 1864).

- Jackson's last words: "Let us cross over the river, and rest under the shade of the trees."

- It was during the Civil War's Battle of Bull Run that Jackson assumed his nickname. Amidst the tumult of battle, Brig. Gen. Barnard E. Bee stated, "There is Jackson standing like a stone wall."

- Jackson appears prominently in the enormous bas-relief carving on the face of Stone Mountain (in Georgia) riding with Jefferson Davis and Robert E. Lee.

- Jackson's steed, Little Sorrel, was the Confederacy's second most famous horse.

- The United States Navy submarine USS *Stonewall Jackson* (SSBN 634), commissioned in 1964, was named for him. Taken from letters written by General Jackson, the words "Strength—Mobility" are emblazoned on the ship's banner.

- Jackson was said to be especially fond of lemons. Visitors frequently leave them at his gravesite. Stonewall Jackson has two separate burial sites. His left arm, which was amputated after the Battle of Chancellorsville, was buried on a nearby farm. A week later, on Sunday, Jackson died and was buried in Lexington, Virginia.